A Special Gift For

_____

With Love

_____

Date

_____

Stories, sayings, and scriptures to Encourage and Inspire

hugs

for Cat Lovers

TAMMY L. BICKET AND
DAWN M. BRANDON

Personalized Scriptures by
LEANN WEISS

HOWARD BOOKS
A DIVISION OF SIMON & SCHUSTER
New York London Toronto Sydney

Our purpose at Howard Books is to:
Increase faith in the hearts of growing Christians
Inspire holiness in the lives of believers
Instill hope in the hearts of struggling people everywhere
Because He's coming again!

Published by Howard Books, a division of Simon & Schuster, Inc.
1230 Avenue of the Americas, New York, NY 10020
www.howardpublishing.com

HOWARD
BOOKS

Hugs for Cat Lovers © 2007 by Tammy L. Bicket and Dawn M. Brandon

Library of Congress Cataloging-in-Publication Data
Bicket, Tammy L.
Hugs for cat lovers / Bicket, Tammy L. and Dawn M. Brandon ; personalized scriptures by LeAnn Weiss.
   p. cm.
   1. Cats—Anecdotes. 2. Cat owners—Anecdotes. 3. Christian life—Miscellanea. I. Brandon, Dawn M. II. Title.
   SF445.5 .B53 2007
   636.8—dc22

                         2007033652

ISBN: 978-1-4767-5143-6

10 9 8 7 6 5 4 3 2 1

Manufactured in the United States of America

For information regarding special discounts for bulk purchases, please contact: Simon & Schuster Special Sales at 1-800-456-6798 or business@simonandschuster.com.

Edited by Chrys Howard
Cover design by Tennille Paden
Interior design by Tennille Paden

Paraphrased scriptures copyright © 2007 by LeAnn Weiss, 3006 Brandywine Drive, Orlando, FL 32806; 407-898-4410

Contents

There are few things in life
more heartwarming than
to be welcomed by a cat.

—Tay Hohoff

CHAPTER ONE

Cats Give Comfort

You can always count on Me! I promise that I'll never leave you or let you down. I'm 100 percent faithful to all of My promises to you. No matter what you're going through, I'm always there when you need help. You'll always find refuge in Me.

Faithfully,
Your Ever-Present God
—*from Proverbs 3:5; Deuteronomy 31:6; Psalm 145:13; 46:1*

Following the death of her mate, Tondalayo was despondent until the coming of a red male tabby cat named T. K. (short for Tonda's Kitten). Her new best friend, the cat raised Tonda's spirits and brought her much-needed comfort. That's not so unusual: that's what cats do, right? Sure, but Tonda is an orangutan at ZooWorld near Panama City Beach in Florida. ZooWorld keepers deliberately gave her the kitten in the hopes that T. K. would provide the comfort their best efforts had been unable to give. Tonda and T. K. share an island and indoor living quarters at the zoo. A *News Herald* feature on the unlikely pair included heartwarming photos of the cat cuddling sweetly with the gigantic ape.

In spite of cats' reputation for being aloof, they can be

acutely perceptive of people's feelings. Often their empathy and kindness confound us. Cats snuggle with us when we're sad. They share our bed, warming our heart and our feet when we're lonely. And some special souls seem to see right through us, greeting us at the door when we've had a particularly rough day, sticking close when we're upset, or gently kneading our legs or our back when we lay across our bed, weeping.

Cat owners are healthier, less stressed, less depressed, and more likely to recover from serious illness than those without pets. Having a cat controls blood pressure better than medication and lowers the risk of heart attack. Perhaps if we had more cats in our lives, we'd need fewer doctors and therapists. And isn't that a comforting thought?

Kittens are angels

with whiskers.

Author unknown

Cat's Cradle

"Play cat's cradle, Mama." The raven-haired four-year-old cherub, tugging firmly on her mother's sleeve, made it sound more like a command than a request. Sienna repressed the sudden urge to grab her daughter and run away—away from the hospital and doctors, away from the gurney that would soon come to take away her precious little Molly to surgery, eight hundred miles away—to Ironwood, Michigan, with family and friends who loved them and where everything would be okay again.

But as she moved to stroke her daughter's hair, her hand brushed against the squirming tyke's abdomen and felt the ominous lump that had brought them to this place. She felt helpless. Surreal. Wild-eyed with fear. And angry: she could feel the anger burning deep inside, but the feeling was trumped by fear that her anger would incur the wrath of God—or was it fate? As if anything she did wrong might somehow make her baby's prognosis even worse. Not that it wasn't bad enough already. Wilms' tumor was cancer, after all— fast-growing—and in her little girl, already quite large. The only questions yet to be answered were what type and what stage was Molly's tumor—oh yes, and would she live to go to kindergarten, learn to read, or grow up?

"Cat's cradle!" Molly demanded impatiently.

Sienna reached into her pocket for the yarn as she checked the clock yet again. *Almost three.* The surgery had been scheduled for noon. *What's taking so long?* "Aren't you tired of this yet?" she asked when Molly squealed in delight as she saw the yarn emerge.

"Do it, Mama! Do it!"

Sienna's hands deftly wove the yarn through her fingers to make the cat's cradle. *Slowly,* she reminded herself. She knew Molly would be watching intently, trying to master the secrets of the game.

"Now me." Molly wiggled with excitement as she tentatively grasped the crossed sections of string between her chubby fingers, pulled them gingerly to the sides, then dove through the sides and tried to come up through the middle to transfer the cat's cradle to her own little hands. But she couldn't quite make it work, and the yarn became one large loop again. Her momentary frustration was replaced with a determined look. "Again." She painstakingly laced the cat's cradle on her own hands under Sienna's watchful eye.

"Mama," Molly said thoughtfully, "Tell me the truth . . ."

Sienna's heart pounded wildly, anticipating a question she didn't want to answer—didn't know how to answer. *Help! Marco!* Her eyes fixed on her husband, dozing in the recliner at the end of the bed. How could he sleep at a time like this? What do you tell a little girl with cancer? How do you find the right answers to whatever tough questions she might ask?

"Why doesn't Angelo like me?"

Sienna's breath returned, and she suppressed a laugh of relief. But Molly was deadly serious.

"He's a cat, Molly," Sienna explained. "Cats don't show affection like people do. He does like you, but he likes you in the way that's natural for cats to like little girls."

"He doesn't like me." Molly shook her head sadly. "Tia's cat, Whiskers, lets Tia pick her up, pet her, hug her, and kiss her. She even sleeps with Tia on her bed. But Angelo won't play with me. He doesn't even want me to touch him." She lowered her gaze dejectedly. "He doesn't like me." Her bottom lip protruded in a pout, quivering slightly in barely controlled sorrow.

Sienna stroked Molly's hair comfortingly and pulled her tighter against her body in a reassuring embrace. She wished it weren't so, but everything Molly said was true.

Angelo had come first—into her life and into her heart. An amazingly large (twenty-five pounds) white Maine coon cat with a thick ruff or mane around his neck and long fur "britches" on his hind legs, the cat had stolen her heart in an instant. But it was his unique eyes—one blue, the other golden—that led her to pronounce him a true work of art and bestow on him the name Michelangelo. She often shortened it to "Angelo," especially when, as a single woman, she had needed a guy to talk about in front of creepy strangers who seemed inclined to ask her out.

Angelo had been the only love of her life for more than two years. He had plainly resented Marco when she started dating him and only begrudgingly adjusted to having him around when they married. Her two "men" coexisted mostly by ignoring each other. But it had been different with Molly. Angelo seemed miffed that Molly had ever been born. Yet Angelo's repulsion was matched just as strongly by Molly's attraction to the big cat. Her main goal in life seemed to be to grab hold of that long, soft fur around Angelo's neck or britches or the little tufts of fur that graced the tops of his ears like a lynx. That silken hair seemed to call to Molly . . . and Angelo answered the call: by hissing when she came near or trilling an offended warning if she managed a fistful of his hair.

Mostly Sienna had felt for Angelo—her companionable cat who had followed her everywhere now made himself scarce to avoid being manhandled. Even now that Molly was getting older, Angelo refused to wait around to see if her touch might grow gentler.

For the first time, Sienna truly empathized with her daughter's unrequited affection for a creature that wanted absolutely nothing to do with her. She rocked Molly back and forth atop the hospital bed. "He may be a little jealous," she said softly. "He was my baby before you were. And he hasn't forgotten how you pulled his hair when you were little."

"I want him to like me," Molly said firmly. "How can I make Angelo like me?"

"Just be patient sweetie, and don't give up."

Two women in scrubs came to take Molly away from her. Sienna clutched the child tightly to her chest, not wanting to let go, kissed her head, and blinked back tears. Then Marco was beside her, stroking Molly's arm sweetly. Too soon their little girl was being wheeled from the room. Sienna leaned on Marco for support but waved and smiled encouragingly at Molly, who looked thoughtful. "I won't give up, Mama," she called back to her. "You'll see."

"Play cat's cradle, Mama?" Molly held up her hands, wrapped in a cat's cradle of red yarn, inviting her mother to transfer it to her own hands.

"If I do, will you try to eat some soup?"

Molly lowered her hands and wrinkled her nose in distaste. "It tastes funny."

"I know, it's the chemo," Sienna empathized. "But you have to eat to keep up your strength." She noted with alarm how pale and thin the little girl was looking three weeks after surgery to remove her right kidney revealed that the cancer had already spread to her lungs. She was one week into a six-month course of intensive chemotherapy, to be followed by radiation. The little girl was already struggling with weakness, sores in her mouth, and nausea. Soon she would lose her lovely black hair. Sienna's throat and eyes burned, and her stomach ached like someone had hit her hard. But she couldn't resist her daughter's eyes imploring her to play. Setting down the lunch tray, she maneuvered the cat's cradle off Molly's fingers and onto her own, much to Molly's satisfaction.

Angelo jumped onto the bed, safely beyond Molly's reach, and sniffed the soup and the mug of milk. Sienna pushed him away and moved the tray to Molly's dresser.

"Now me," Molly announced, preparing to try to take back the yarn handiwork.

"Later," Sienna said firmly. "Let's take a look at your incision."

Obligingly, Molly pulled up her nightgown. Sienna was startled again at the sight of the PICC line hanging from her daughter's chest. Inserted during surgery to make chemotherapy easier, it was a constant reminder of what she so desperately wanted to forget: her daughter was deathly ill. Under the bandage she inspected the curved incision that stretched from hip to hip. The first time she'd seen it, Molly had remarked that it looked like a giant smile; but from Sienna's perspective it was an angry, taunting frown.

After a few spoonfuls of soup, Molly vomited the paltry

contents of her stomach and lay weakly on the bed. Sienna had to prop her head up to help her rinse her mouth with water. By the time she got back from cleaning up, Molly had fallen into an exhausted sleep.

Sienna sat at the foot of the bed and watched her, praying silently. The desperation and fear soon morphed back into the old anger she'd tried hard to suppress. Although Molly's cancer was a devastating stage IV, doctors gave her a 90 percent chance of surviving four years—but that left a 10 percent chance her daughter would die soon. And even if she was in that 90 percent, what then? What were the odds she'd live to ten? To twenty? To a ripe old age? It wasn't fair. She wanted more for Molly!

How can You do this to me? She railed in her heart against God. *How could You let this happen? Why do You let my beautiful child suffer?* She felt the comforting warmth of Angelo against her back as she sobbed her frustration out to God. *Do You care? Are You there? Why do You feel so far away when I need You to be close?*

In anguish Sienna retreated to her own bedroom, fell to her knees by her bed, buried her face in her comforter to muffle the sound, and sobbed until she lay exhausted across a bed wet with tears. In the silence that followed, she felt impressed to go to the Bible. Digging it out of her nightstand drawer, she flipped to Psalm 91 and read: "He will command his angels concerning you to guard you in all your ways. . . . He will call upon me, and I will answer him; I will be with him in trouble." For the first time in a long time, she felt a measure of peace. She finally felt hopeful of God's presence. But were there really angels guarding her sick little girl?

She was drawn to Molly's room to check on her. What Sienna saw made her catch her breath. Angelo was snuggled up under Molly's arm as she slept—stretched out the entire length of her body. His watchful eyes followed Sienna's movements, but he made no attempt to go to her as he normally would. Instead, he purred loudly and contentedly in spite of the fact that the sleeping, smiling little girl was grasping a fistful of his long white hair.

And Sienna felt absolutely certain that this "cat in the cradle" was an "angel" sent by God to remind her that He was there.

CHAPTER TWO

Cats Kindle Hope

I will comfort you in heartache and loss. Watch Me rebuild your life, bringing beauty out of the ashes. The enemy is out to rob and ruin you; but I sent My Son to give you abundant life. My love will fill your heart with the hope that never disappoints.

Caring for you,
Your Heavenly Father
—from Isaiah 61:2–4; John 10:10; Romans 5:5

A baby is God's way of saying the world should go on. So is a kitten. Her sweet little face, unsteady movements, and ethereal voice can melt even the hardest of hearts. But going beyond appearance, a kitten is a bundle of promise, potential, possibilities, and hope. We can only imagine what she might become—how large, how powerful, how graceful and dignified. We must wait to see who she becomes, her likes and dislikes, her special gifts, unique personality, and endearing traits. Might she be a champion? Will she be an explorer, a scrapper, or a contented homebody?

We watch our kittens grow with anticipation—eager for what's ahead, not sad for what's lost. Although we look back fondly, maybe even wistfully at what once was, we don't feel sad. For life is about change. No change means no growth, no surprises, no delights.

Just as we must say good-bye to the kitten if we are to make the acquaintance of the cat, so we must let go of the past if we are to embrace the future. Ecclesiastes 7:10 says, "Don't always be asking, 'Where are the good old days?' Wise folks don't ask questions like that" (MSG).

Without the rain, there are no rainbows. The sun is most glorious when piercing storm clouds. From death comes new life; from the ashes of loss, God brings beauty. He always plans a second act, so there's hope for your tomorrow.

Cats' whiskers are so sensitive,
they can find their way
through the narrowest crack
in a broken heart.

Author unknown

Cataclysm

Something big was coming. He could feel it. Mat eyed the darkening horizon with a mixture of anticipation and anxiety. After the long, hot drought, a good soaker would be welcome relief. But he wasn't sure the old barn could withstand a strong storm, and that's what the ominous clouds gathering over the next hill seemed to portend. He eased the old pickup over the crest of the hill. He'd always loved the view from there of his little bit of land. The trees obscured the barn, but he could see the open spot where the old farmhouse had stood. He hoped to build a new cabin on that old foundation, but somehow there never seemed to be enough time or money. There could have been, he knew that. But he never had the heart to turn away the many stray, injured, or orphaned animals that found their way to his door, so most of his money and time went to caring for them.

Over the years he'd cared for all kinds of critters. But cats remained his favorites: their unique personalities delighted and amused him. At least a dozen felines roamed freely throughout the barn, each with a name and a special place in his heart. They were his companions, his family. And each evening, when he retired to the roughly finished loft, a motley assortment of felines always awaited him. Some lounged on the bed, grooming. Others crouched down, eying any mouse that dared to wander in. And most always, Patch would be curled up in the soft chair, one leg stretched out at an impossible angle, head upside down.

As Mat drove, he couldn't help but notice the odd formation the clouds were taking. They were billowing and drifting, but not like the rest of the clouds. And they were darker. Sooty.

Understanding dawned. That wasn't a storm cloud. It was smoke.

Mat's heart seemed to stop. His thoughts were frozen into a vague shape of dread and denial. But as he floored the gas pedal and sped home, the fears swiftly took shape. He tried to stay calm and rational. Maybe it was just a grass fire nearby. He hoped so. But his sinking heart felt the truth. *The barn . . . all the animals!* He jerked the steering wheel and swung onto the dirt road. The truck creaked and rattled and sounded as if it would fall apart as Mat raced on, leaving a thick cloud of dust that obscured everything behind him nearly as completely as the thick cloud of smoke obscured what was ahead.

He skidded to a stop and ran toward the flaming structure. He knew it wasn't safe to go in. But he couldn't just stand outside and let everything—his life's work, the animals who depended on him, the only family he had left—be incinerated before his eyes. He barely noticed the sirens except to realize that he hadn't thought to call 911. But there was no time now. If there was anything left of his little world, he had only seconds to save it.

Pulling the neckline of his T-shirt up over his nose and mouth to try to keep out the smoke, he coughed and squinted and felt his way up the stairs to the loft. His once comfortable room was engulfed in flame and the blackest, thickest smoke he'd ever seen. He felt for the chair only to find it covered in roofing that had already begun to collapse. He tried to move it, searching for Patch and any other cat who might have been trapped underneath. Heat and pain seared his hands, and though he'd tried to hold his breath, now he was choking. Suddenly he wasn't sure he could make it out. He turned and was stumbling down the steps when he felt the boards give out, and he came crashing down.

"Mat . . ." He thought he heard his name above the clatter of boards and the roar of the fire.

"MAT!!" Even the shout sounded strangely muffled, and he couldn't answer. But he felt strong, gloved hands grip his ankles and drag him out as everything faded to black.

When he opened his eyes, he was lying in the hospital with an oxygen mask strapped to his face. He reached up to remove it, only to find both of his hands bandaged and of no help whatsoever. A middle-aged man with soot on his face and a bloody gash on his forehead brought back the realization of what had happened. Mat had known Ben for nearly forty years, since they were boys.

"Better leave that on." Ben sat down in the chair, the lines of exhaustion on his face showing even through the soot, avoiding Mat's eyes as he spoke. "Thought for a minute there we'd lost ya."

Mat nodded. "Who pulled me out?" He paused. "It was you, wasn't it?" Mat knew Ben wouldn't have sent any of his team into a building that far gone.

Ben just unfolded his arms and leaned forward with his elbows on his knees. He took a deep breath. "The boys are still out there, makin' sure the animals in the outside pens are all okay and that the fire doesn't spread."

Mat could feel the tears welling up in his eyes, and he looked away, overwhelmed by his friend's brave and selfless risk but also by the crushing realization of what Ben's words meant.

"It's all gone, isn't it."

Ben kept his head down, but nodded. "I'll go out there when it cools down and see if I can find anything."

Mat swallowed hard and drew a ragged breath. "Thanks." But he knew it was all gone—his records, the photos and video of his animals through the years . . . every recorded memory and evidence of his life and work was in ashes. Everything he had in this world had burned, and now it seemed that not only his past but his present and his future had gone up in smoke.

"You, uh . . ." Mat clenched his jaw to regain control of his breaking voice. "Haven't seen Patch anywhere, have you?"

Ben gave his friend a miserable, silent look. Matt sniffed and nodded briskly. "Well," he said gruffly to hide his emotion. "When can I go ho—"

What did it matter? The question was pointless. He could never go home again.

Ben made one final tromp through the ashes of Mat's place. He paused; did he hear something?

He moved to where several boards had tumbled together at odd angles. There it was again. But it couldn't be.

Mew.

Just one short, faint sound, but this time Ben was certain he'd heard it.

Mew.

Carefully he sifted through the pile, moving one board at a time. At last, in a tiny pocket at the very bottom, he spotted two little eyes peering up at him. He lay down, reached in, and pulled up a tiny kitten. "Well, well . . . how in the world did you get here, and how did you survive a fire like that?" The poor kitten was badly singed, and since it had been trapped for several days, Ben knew it might be too late to save it. But he'd try. "You're a little miracle, that's for sure," Ben told the kitten. He tucked it under his arm to drive to the veterinary hospital. "Let's see if we can't work another miracle for Mat."

When Ben picked up Mat to take him "home" from the hospital, the future still felt bleak. "You can stay with me till you get your new place," Ben had offered generously. Mat wondered if Ben knew what he was getting himself into. He had no new place lined up; no money to rent, buy, or build one.

"Need you to stop by your place first," Ben informed Mat as he drove. "Need to check in on things." The men rode in silence, Mat staring glumly into the side rearview mirror, watching a much smaller, fainter dust trail than the last time he'd driven this road. At long last the rain had come. *The day after my barn and all my critters burned*, he thought bitterly.

He leaned his head back and closed his eyes, trying to brace himself for what he'd see. Even when Ben stopped the truck, Mat didn't stir. But a vague commotion made him open his eyes.

Mat's jaw dropped as he took in the scene. There, on the site of the old farmhouse, was the half-constructed frame of a small cabin. At least twenty people were scurrying around, waving and smiling as they worked. Mat's eyes filled with tears, and he felt a sharp pain in his throat. He glanced over at Ben, who had shifted to lean against the truck door, one arm resting on top of the steering wheel. When Ben looked at him with that old sly smirk, Mat felt the corner of his mouth quiver, and he had to look away.

"What—" Mat couldn't finish.

"You can't—I can't—"

"Oh yes you can, and you will." Ben opened the door and got out of the truck. "What are you waitin' for, the grass to grow? Go have a look!"

Mat surveyed the project in amazement. It was too much to take in. He rounded the corner and suddenly was face to face with the old barn site. Ben stepped up behind him and silently handed him a roll of paper. Mat unrolled it to see rough plans for a new barn.

"It's just a sketch," Ben said. "You can figure out just how you want it and what you need to make it a proper shelter. But the building materials will be supplied, and as you can see, we've got plenty of skilled labor."

Mat's mouth was agape again when he turned to speak to Ben, who seemed to be hiding something.

"There's something else I want to show you," Ben said with a grin. From behind his back he produced a tiny, dark gray ball of fur. "Found him under the rubble of the old barn," he said, handing the kitten with bandaged paws to Mat and indicating his friend's still-bandaged hands. "Figure you're a matched set. He needs someone to nurse him back to health, and I was hoping you'd take him on as your first patient."

"Well, Smokey," Mat said, promptly naming his new ward. "It seems life goes on after all. I hope you like bein' 'round lotsa other critters." He gently stroked the kitten's chin as it purred and curled up contentedly in the crook of his arm.

Mat couldn't help but laugh, and as he did, the tears he'd been trying to hold back spilled onto his cheeks. He brushed them away quickly with the back of his bandaged hand and turned back toward the few remaining ashes as the wind did its best to swirl them around like smoke, only to have them settle back down again, no match for the bright afternoon sunshine.

CHAPTER THREE

Cats Inspire

Even before you were born, I scheduled your days. When you face opposition and obstacles, remember the possibilities because I am for you. You can make a difference because I strengthen you. Use wisdom, thinking outside the box to make the most of every opportunity.

Guiding you daily,
Your Wise Provider
—*from Psalm 139:16; Mark 10:27; Romans 8:31; Philippians 4:13; Colossians 4:5*

There's just something about cats and creative types. History is full of innovative people who loved cats as much as ingenuity. Scientist Isaac Newton, wanting to ensure that his cats would be able to wander freely in and out as he worked, invented the cat flap. Nobel Peace Prize winner Dr. Albert Schweitzer learned to write with his right hand so he wouldn't have to awaken his cat Sizi when she fell asleep on his left arm. Another cat, Piccolo, slept on the papers on Dr. Schweitzer's desk. Visionary statesman Winston Churchill was particularly fond of Jock, an orange tabby who attended cabinet meetings.

The connection seems especially strong with writers. Ernest Hemingway had thirty cats. Harriet Beecher Stowe's cat, Calvin, often sat on her shoulder as she wrote. Thomas Hardy, Lewis Carroll, Beatrix

Potter, William Butler Yeats, and H. G. Wells were avid cat lovers, as was Mark Twain. Twain's daughter Susy once remarked, "Mamma loves morals and Papa loves cats." Charles Dickens kept a much-loved kitten in his study for company when he wrote. When she wanted his attention, she would put out his candle.

Perhaps the fascination for creative types is that they see in cats kindred spirits: nonconforming originals with a penchant for surprising people. All cat lovers have their own stories about the intelligence and ingenuity of a favorite feline learning to flush the toilet, finding a way to open drawers and cupboards, or working their way into hearts most hardened to their charms. Cats are smart, outside-the-box thinkers—and, in loving them, so are you.

Authors like cats because they are such quiet, lovable, wise creatures, and cats like authors for the same reasons.

Robertson Davies

Cat Tales

Sharon sat on the cold stone steps in front of the old library as autumn leaves swirled and caught in the corners. "That's how I feel," she said glumly to the cat rubbing against her legs. "Swept aside and trapped in a corner." She let out a sigh and stroked the cat's head, evoking a loud, purring meow.

"I sure would miss our little morning visits." She dabbed at the tears gathering in her eyes. "So far, just about the only new patron I've been able to attract is you. And how many books have you checked out lately?" she asked in mock sternness. In coy reply, her furry friend rolled over at her feet and exposed his belly for a gentle rub. "You know I'd take you home with me if I could, but that mean old landlord won't let me," she cooed. The cat rolled to his feet, yawned, and stretched out his chin for a scratch. Sharon smiled sadly. "It sure would be nice to

have some company—it gets awfully lonely there all by myself."
She swallowed and tried to pull herself together. It was nearly
opening time.

"All right," she said, getting to her feet. "I really do have to
get in there—today's the big day, you know." She rose and took in
the view of the red brick, Victorian Gothic building with its cross
gables and tall, narrow windows. She loved that building, loved the
smell of old wood and old books inside.

She fumbled with the key in the stiff lock, then tugged at one
of the two heavy oak doors. The cat had been doing figure eights
around and between her legs, as he did every morning before
meandering off behind the thick northern bayberries on either side
of the entryway. But today, before the door was open more than a
few inches, he darted inside.

Sharon gasped in surprise and consternation. "You little dickens!
Come back here!"

She rushed inside, plunked her purse and lunch bag on the
reference desk, and took off in the direction the cat had disappeared.
"Here, kitty, kitty." She hadn't allowed herself to name him,
forbidding herself to become emotionally attached to a companion
she couldn't keep. But she knew it was in vain. The gregarious
brown marbled feline had won her over instantly.

"Kiiiiitty, kitty, kitty," she called. The fugitive was nowhere to
be seen.

"You couldn't have picked a worse day for this, you know—the photographer will be here any minute!" She glanced nervously at the clock.

A movement near the reference section caught her eye, but by the time she got there, the cat had vanished back into the shadows. She walked briskly up and down the rows and just glimpsed him slinking around the corner to the fiction shelves. "Oh," she groaned. "I'll never find you in there!" The dark mix of colors in his fur would be the perfect disguise against the chestnut shelves.

"Please," she begged, her lips quivering as her desperation grew. "You can't be in here—this photo shoot is my last hope of getting some publicity and bringing in more visitors." *And keeping my job*, she thought miserably. "Why does *everything* have to go wrong?!" She cast an accusing look heavenward—and found herself looking at two glowing eyes. Sepia and flecked with green, they gave the impression of aged copper. "There you are!"

Sharon had to admit, the cat looked as though he belonged exactly there, curled contentedly on the top shelf, next to *Great Expectations*. She spoke to the cat softly and in soothing tones. "Now, I'm gonna pull this nice little stool over and come up to your level, okay?"

Meow.

Sharon moved slowly so as not to startle him. She stroked his cheek as he purred, then slowly moved her hand down his side. "Come here, baby." She scooped him up gently, and to her surprise, he offered no resistance or objection. "Well, are you used to being cuddled?" She stroked his head as she stepped down from the stool. "How did a sweet little fellow like you come to be wandering around—"

"Oh!" She had turned toward the front entry and was startled to see a boy standing near the door. "Hello," she said brightly. "Can I help you?" She knew the handful of children who came regularly to the library, but this was a new face.

"I came to see the cat," he said shyly.

"Excuse me?" Sharon said, puzzled.

"I saw him come in," he answered, pointing at the furry bundle in Sharon's left arm, "and I wanted to see the cat in the library."

Sharon chuckled and squatted so he could pet the cat. "He snuck in with me this morning. I was just taking him back outside." She stood and moved toward the door. "Want to come with me and see him off?"

The boy followed, and the three of them stepped out into the sunlight.

Snap, snap, snap, snap.

The photographer had already started taking pictures.

"Good morning," Sharon said, a little flustered. "It's a lovely building, isn't it?"

The man smiled warmly. "Nothing like the old style. What's his name?" he said, giving a half nod at her furry cargo.

"Oh!" She gave a nervous laugh as she realized she was still holding the cat and released him. "Um . . ." She thought quickly, remembering her earlier epithet and the shelf where she'd found the little stowaway. "Dickens," she said with a grin, then offered her hand in greeting. "I'm Sharon Sterling, the librarian. If you've got what you need out here, come in, and I'll show you some great reasons for people to visit our library."

Sharon could hardly wait to see the newspaper feature. She'd worked hard soliciting local art and historical photographs of the area, and she'd stayed up until the wee hours of the morning arranging the displays and making everything perfect. The library board had made it clear that if this final effort didn't work, they would have no choice but to close the library.

So that morning she rushed inside, plopped down eagerly behind the circulation desk, and opened the newspaper. But what she saw burst her last bubble of hope.

The photographer hadn't used any shots of the displays she'd prepared so carefully. No pictures of the glorious antique shelving or even of the comfortable new seating area she'd convinced the board to let her add. No photos of the brightly decorated children's section with its "Take a reading adventure!" travel theme. Instead, the photographer had chosen just one photo of the outside of the building, which anyone could see from the street.

But it got worse.

Splashed across the front page of the Community section was an 8 x 6 photo of the library entrance—showing Sharon with the shy boy . . . and Dickens the cat. The huge, sure-to-be-career-killing headline read: "Library cat draws new, young visitors."

"Ugh," she slapped her hand to her forehead. "They're gonna kill me."

"But Mr. Churlton, please try to understand," Sharon pleaded into the phone receiver. "I never meant for Dickens to be the library's cat—"

"Yes, sir, I know there are health regulations—"

"No, I didn't seek the board's approval, but if you'll just let me explain, that's because—"

She winced at the angry click that ended her conversation with the head of the library board, his final, bellowing command echoing in her ears: *Get rid of that cat!*

Sharon slumped in her chair and let her head sink down into

her hands. She didn't know which loss would break her heart more: her library job or the library cat, both of which she loved dearly.

"Miss Sterling?" said a timid little voice. "Where's the kitty?"

"Oh," she let out a weary sigh. "I don't know, Keenan. Let's go see if we can find him." They went outside and called for Dickens, who emerged at his leisure from the bayberries but rewarded their patience with a rub and a merry meow. Keenan's face lit up, dispelling some of the darkness of Sharon's mood.

"I'll come see you again tomorrow, Dickens," Keenan promised. "I wish I had a cat like you," he said wistfully.

"You do, do you?" Sharon reached down and offered her hand in service to Dickens for a cheek rub. Since they'd met the day Dickens sneaked into the library, Keenan and Dickens had become fast friends. "Well, Dickens sure seems to like you."

Sharon looked at Keenan and cocked her head. An idea was growing.

Sharon was putting the finishing touches on the library bulletin board when she noticed a child standing behind her. "Oh, hello, Keenan. How's Dickens today?"

"Purr-fect!" Keenan said emphatically.

Sharon giggled. "Want to help me put up the last picture?"

She helped Keenan onto the library stool and gave him a pushpin. "Right about . . . there. Now *this* is purr-fect." She tousled the boy's hair and grinned.

She turned back to the display with a smile, savoring the evidence of how far she and the library had come in the past year: photographs of adult readers absorbed in novels and overstuffed chairs; snapshots of kids taking grand adventures on the Reading Railway she'd painted on the floor; and the brand-new young adult reading room, with its neon light over the doorway and several junior-high and high-schoolers at the monthly After-Hours Teen Night.

She'd gotten off to a rough start, but with a little out-of-the-box thinking, she'd managed to turn things around . . . with a little help, of course. Help that showed up in every single photo of library visitors: an officially appointed, board-sanctioned, brown marbled library cat.

Whether curled contentedly inside a visitor's open briefcase, playing energetically with the youngest library members, or with coppery eyes glowing amid his teenaged nocturnal company, Dickens basked in his rightful place at the center of attention. His overwhelming popularity (and pressure from a few cat-loving patrons) had convinced even Mr. Churlton to let him move inside, where he made his private quarters atop what everyone now called the Dickens shelf. But during library hours, he was on duty in

Acquisitions (bringing in new visitors), Circulation (making the rounds among readers), and Administration (which looked a lot like napping).

Sharon glanced over at the children's section to see Dickens lounging on a nearby shelf, purring contentedly as he allowed each small visitor a turn at stroking his fur.

"Come on, Keenan, let's join the story circle. Today's book is *Puss in Boots*. I just love a good cat tale!"

CHAPTER FOUR

Cats Bring Peace

ursue peace. I'll bless you when you are a peacemaker. Come to Me in prayer with your worries, and you'll experience My peace that surpasses all understanding.

Loving you always,
Your Prince of Peace

—from Psalm 34:14; Matthew 5:9; Philippians 4:6–7; Isaiah 9:6

If you've ever seen a Bengal cat, you won't soon forget it. This unique and beautiful creature is the product of crossing a domestic cat with a wild leopard cat native to Southeast Asia. Bengals' spotted markings strongly resemble leopards', and the cats—especially first-generation Bengals—have a markedly wild look that softens with subsequent generations. But they share a softer side with the domestic cat. They're friendly and outgoing, even enjoying playing in water or a quick game of fetch.

Bringing together two vastly different—even conflicting—parties could be explosive; but instead, the benefits are surprising. Bengal cats are exceptionally healthy and intelligent precisely because of this blending.

If you've ever been caught

between two sides in an argument or family feud, you won't soon forget that either. It may be tempting to run away, duck, or choose a side and jump in with guns blazing. But such responses do nothing to tame the wild beasts of discord that threaten to devour us along with those we love when they fight. They only inflame the anger and strife.

Instead, we can be the Bengal cats of our world, bringing two disparate, warring parties together in peaceful coexistence. Seeing both sides, being quick to listen but slow to condemn, responding calmly and rationally without becoming inflamed, and being willing to sacrifice our time and what's best for ourselves for the good of others: these are some ways we can help make peace between the wild cats in our lives. "Blessed are the peacemakers," the Bible says, "for they will be called sons of God" (Matthew 5:9).

Most people are just like cats in that if you rub them the right way, they will purr. But if you rub them the wrong way, they will bite and scratch.

William Ross

Cat Fight

"Watch it!" Charlie nervously pushed a loose strand of her wavy auburn hair behind her ear and hovered protectively as the movers awkwardly maneuvered her prized possession, a quilt-wrapped baby grand piano, through the woefully inadequate front door of her woefully tiny new house. She heard it thud against the doorjamb, heard discordant notes from deep within and then the muffled plunk of individual notes as one mover's fingers found the keyboard.

"Be careful," Charlie pleaded, miserable but feeling powerless to help. The piano was way bigger than she was, and there just wasn't room for one more person to help thread the needle. It was nerve-wracking to watch . . . and exhausting. She felt like throwing up her hands and running away when she added this newest stress to all the wearying, frustrating issues and tasks she'd been dealing with alone for the past month with the move—and the past eighteen months with the messy divorce. Charlie was more than ready for a break—for some peace and quiet. But that would have to wait until after she unpacked more boxes than seemed likely to fit in her new little Cape Cod charmer—with the emphasis on *little* rather than *charm.*

When the beefy men finally got the bulky piano through the narrow opening and set it down just inside the door, Charlie was shocked to see how much of the front room it swallowed up. *That's okay,* she thought dryly. *Then I won't have to buy much furniture to replace what "Ratboy" took.*

She directed them as they moved, adjusted, and readjusted the piano to find the perfect spot for it—where she'd be able to see out either window when she played for pleasure and still have room for a chair beside the piano bench where she could sit and monitor her piano students' progress when she used the piano for her work. The men started to unwrap the piano, but she stopped them. That was something she wanted to do herself. She noticed the ubiquitous blond cat hairs on the dark quilts and briefly wondered how her feline trio—Jazz, Minuet, and Tango—was doing locked in the back bedroom. She knew the move would be upsetting for them, but hey, why should she be the only one? At least they didn't have to unpack boxes.

After carefully inspecting the piano and finding a couple of minor nicks and scratches, she sat down to make sure it still played okay. "Ouch," she winced. The move had knocked it terribly out of tune. She'd expected as much: she'd already scheduled the tuner to come the next day. Her thoughts were interrupted by the ringing of the phone. *Why didn't I wait a few days to have that connected?* Charlie thought ruefully as she saw on the caller ID that it was her older sister.

"Hi, Georgie," Charlie tried to sound pleasant. "Calling to wish me luck in my new home?"

"Did you know they're going on another date?" Georgie's tone was condemning.

"Who, Dad?" Charlie asked wearily.

"And that gold-digging woman no older than I am." She paused, but barely. "And Mom gone just four months. It's unseemly."

Charlie sighed and thought again about running away. "He's lonely. He probably just needs someone to talk to."

"Then why doesn't he talk to me?" Georgeanne demanded.

Maybe he would if you were sweeter to him. Charlie wisely refrained from sharing the thought. "Look, the movers are still here, and things are really hopping. I'll have to talk to you later."

She'd barely put down the phone when it rang again. She saw that it was her younger sister, Andie, and this time she didn't answer.

Charlie awoke in the black of night to find herself upright in bed, her heart pounding. Had she heard a bloodcurdling scream, or had she dreamed it? She'd anticipated that her first night in the new house would be a bit creepy with unfamiliar noises, creaks, and groans, but this was no house noise—it was terrifying! She clutched the bedsheet to her chest and listened: There it was again . . . inside the house. The cats. Something was terribly wrong. What could it be?

She jumped out of bed and ran toward the sounds, not even pausing when she jammed her toe on a box at the foot of the bed. She wished she could grab a baseball bat, but she had no idea in which box anything was packed. She could hear hissing and a strange high-pitched, threatening "singing" she'd never heard before. Was one of the cats hurt? Lovesick? Were they facing down a vicious axe murderer? Maybe she should be running in the opposite direction. But curiosity and fear for her cats drove Charlie around the corner and into the music room. Minuet and Tango dashed past her, seeking cover while Jazz—looking inflated to twice her normal size—confronted a dark and shadowy intruder alone. The uninvited cat saw Charlie coming, turned tail, and scooted through the kitchen and out the pet door, hotly pursued by a cream-colored she-devil that had once been Charlie's diminutive, sweet companion, Jazz.

Quickly blocking the pet door with the piece of board in the garage she finally realized was intended for that purpose, Charlie went to check on Jazz and the others. It took quite a while for Jazz's fur to relax and for her to return to normal size, but though she was tense, she seemed uninjured. It took even longer to find Tango and Minuet in their various hiding spots; neither could be coaxed out. But they didn't seem damaged. Charlie breathed a sigh of relief. It was over.

But it wasn't. Her cats' midnight encounter with the interloper had changed them. Instead of standing together against a threat they easily could have handled as a group, they turned on one another. They simply could not be together without erupting into a replay of that fateful night—only this time they were attacking one another, forgetting they were on the same side . . . sisters.

As the weeks turned into months of incessant sparring, she desperately followed any advice from cat experts. She'd tried bathing the cats to get any residual smell of the intruder off of them. She had the carpets shampooed and scrubbed down the walls and baseboards. She used room deodorizers and even sprayed perfume and different powders on the cats to make them smell alike and less threatening. But she found she just had to keep them separated when she wasn't right there to supervise, and even then the fur often flew. She understood that the newness of the place and the timing of the unfortunate incident added to the difficulty in recovering, but she couldn't change what had happened. She couldn't undo it; couldn't go back to the old home even if she wanted to. The cats were just going to have to adjust and learn to get along once more. She wondered if there would ever be peace again.

"Andie . . . Andie, please. I've got to go!" Charlie pleaded with her younger sister. "That was the doorbell. My three-o'clock is here early. I'll call you later." She didn't have time to round up the cats and send them to their separate rooms. She hoped they'd be on their best behavior for the half-hour lesson.

Charlie didn't feel like making small talk or feigning a pleasant mood. She was grateful her student was a twelve-year-old boy who practiced much and talked little. He played the minor strains of Beethoven's "Für Elise," an emotionally fertile backdrop for her to rehash her conversation with her sister. She didn't want to be in the middle of their battles. Ever since her widowed father had remarried—six months after their mother died, and to a woman twenty-three years his junior—her family had been in turmoil.

She understood her sisters' concern: when their father died, would all of their mother's things—family heirlooms, sentimental keepsakes, their rightful inheritance—be lost to their family forever by passing to a woman who would likely live as long as they did? Still, there was no call for the sniping that had developed between the sisters. Why did they each insist that Charlie take their side in their petty squabbles? What did that accomplish except to push them further apart? It was as pointless and as stupid as the way her cats were acting. She wryly acknowledged how much the relationship among her sisters resembled the cat fights that were wearing her out at home. She wished she could figure a way out of her miserable dilemmas, but she felt powerless again. Still.

Out of the corner of her eye, Charlie could see it developing, but it unfolded too fast for her to do anything about it. Her largest cat, the red tabby Tango, was headed straight for the smaller but feisty dominant cat, Jazz. The two neared each other with bloodlust in their eyes and their teeth bared. Charlie sucked in her breath and braced for the carnage but was startled to see a flash move between the two combatants. Although she had moved quickly, the wiry, lanky, red-ticked Minuet seemed relaxed and oblivious to the danger as she casually inserted herself in the center of the fray. *Look out, you clueless cat!* Charlie's mind screamed silent warnings to the gentle Minuet. *You'll be killed!*

But Jazz and Tango pulled up short, temporarily deflected from their murderous mission. They tried to move around Minuet, but clumsily she seemed always to be right where they were headed.

Although irritated with Min, neither Jazz nor Tango seemed to have the stomach for battling her.

As her piano student, oblivious, switched to playing Bach's sprightly Minuet in G, Charlie was amazed to see a gradual change. While Min stood between them, Jazz started grooming herself and Tango calmly walked away. The encounter was over. Peace had won.

Charlie's spirit soared with the music. New admiration for Minuet and greater understanding came to her. It was possible to avoid being drawn into a battle without avoiding the combatants. Minuet had stood between feuding sisters and brought peace. With a renewed sense of compassion and commitment, Charlie resolved to find a way to stand between her sisters—and bring peace.

It had been a good lesson.

CHAPTER FIVE

Cats Are Worth the Investment

Generous giving doubles as an investment in your future. When you give, I will bless you in even greater ways. Be confident that you'll experience My goodness as you wait on Me. And don't forget that I love to abundantly exceed your expectations and your biggest dreams.

Blessing you back,
Your Source of Every Good Gift
—*from Ecclesiastes 11:1; Luke 6:38; Psalm 27:13–14; Ephesians 3:20; James 1:17*

Loving a cat can be expensive! Despite the fact that 70 percent of cats are obtained at no initial cost, getting a cat is just the tip of the iceberg. Between paying for spaying or neutering, vaccinations, food, litter, medical care, treats, toys, bedding, boarding, scratching posts, and grooming, your expenditures for your cat may reach a thousand dollars a year—or more! And that's not including the cost of shredded drapes and chairs, carpet cleaning (or replacement), room deodorizers, cat doors, and all those cures for hairballs and gadgets for removing shed hair.

Caring for a feline friend isn't cheap, but any true cat lover will tell you without a moment's hesitation: it's worth every penny. Providing for a cat is a truly wise investment. Although we humans are the partners who put up all the cold, hard cash, this furry "business partner" pays warm, soft dividends of the very best kind. Who can buy anything as gratifying as having a cat purr happily in response to your touch? No rich man can afford a more noble or loyal companion than you earn when you treat your cat with kindness and respect. Give a cat your all—your enthusiasm, your affection, your devotion, your time, and your heart—and everything you give will be returned to you. Your cat will entertain, inspire, edify, educate, enlighten, and love you. So go ahead and spend yourself on behalf of a cat today. It's always worth the investment.

When you're special to a cat, you're special indeed . . . she brings to you the gift of her preference of you, the sight of you, the sound of your voice, the touch of your hand.

Leonore Fleisher

Cat's Eye

"Mom, come quick!" Fourteen-year-old Skye Thomas burst breathlessly through the front door on the first day of summer vacation. "Jinxy's after two kittens. I'm afraid he'll kill them!" She raced back outside, knowing Mom would follow. No one loved animals—especially cats—more than her mother.

"Where are they?" Mom asked curtly as they scanned the area for the neighborhood bully cat and its hapless victims.

"I don't know," Skye said worriedly. "One kitten went that way, and the other went toward Kunzes' house with Jinx hot on its tail." They ran across the street in the direction of the pursued feline.

The uneasy calm was shattered by a bloodcurdling "scream." It was coming from under a souped-up white pickup—parked in front of the "party house"—with tires so small Skye marveled that anything could fit beneath it. She'd often seen it drive through the neighborhood, loud music rattling its windows, its bumper scraping the street. Dashing around to the front of the truck, Skye startled the large white cat, the hairs on its enormous black and gray ringed tail standing straight out like a toilet brush. But Jinx—tail flicking with tension—didn't abandon his post or shift his focus from under the truck until Skye's mom flew into range. Jinx had tangled with Bryn Thomas before. The moment he saw her, he abandoned his quarry and melted away faster than ice on a sizzling-hot grill—and with about as much hissing and spitting.

"Go home, Jinx!" Mom hollered. "Bad cat!"

Skye crouched and turned practically on her head trying to see the object of the bully cat's wrath. Two wide green eyes stared back at her, and the kitten emitted a high-pitched, tiny mew as it tumbled out into the open like a floppy rag doll.

"Ohhh," Skye murmured affectionately as the little brown spotted tabby tried to scramble up the leg of her jeans.

"It's adorable!" Mom cooed. "And so trusting and friendly."

Skye lifted the soft, warm body into her arms. It weighed almost nothing, and she could feel its ribs. Still, the soothing vibrations of its purring relaxed her as it rubbed its face against her hand. "I think it knows we rescued it," she said softly. "It's saying thank you."

"Look, here comes its brother or sister." Her mom pointed out a blue-swirled tabby scampering across the street from the safety of the Hayneses' bushes. It had longer hair than the first kitten and seemed just as eager for human contact. Skye's mom scooped it up. "I wonder where they came from. Have you seen them around before?"

Skye nodded. "I saw them a few days ago when I was riding my bike. They ran after me, and I was afraid I was going to run them over."

Skye's mom frowned. "They seem starved for affection— and food, too. He's pretty thin. I wonder if anyone's caring for them."

As if on cue, a motorcycle rumbled into the driveway at party house, and a young, helmetless man wearing a Napalm Death concert T-shirt got off, removed his sunglasses, and hung them on the neck of his shirt. A tattoo of a snake came to life when his bicep flexed. He was looking at them.

"I see you've met Heineken," he nodded toward the kitten Skye's mother held, "and Budweiser." He glanced in Skye's direction and smiled a surprisingly pleasant smile.

"Are these your kittens?" Skye's mother asked boldly.

"Are now."

"They seem rather young and vulnerable to be left outside on their own all day."

"Done fine so far."

"My daughter nearly ran them over with her bike the other day," she pressed. "And today they were attacked by a much larger cat." She waited for some response.

"Cat fight." He seemed thoughtful. "Cool."

Skye could sense her mother's righteous indignation rising and waited for the fireworks.

"I do hope you'll take proper care of your cats," she said with civility, although the warning was clear. "It's against the law not to take proper care of animals."

"I take care of 'em," he protested. He pointed to the porch of the house. "Put out food and water every day."

Her mom examined the brown kitten in Skye's arms and frowned. "Looks like this kitten was scratched when he was attacked. His left eye seems irritated. Cat scratches often become infected," she warned. "He really ought to be checked by a vet."

"Snake" didn't look happy, Skye thought. He snatched the cats and headed abruptly for his house. "My roommate's a vet," he called over his shoulder glibly. "Lucky thing." With that, he and the kittens disappeared behind the windowless door.

Skye had seen Snake's roommates. She was pretty sure neither was a vet.

The veterinary office smelled like a peculiar combination of antiseptic and wet fur. Skye smiled back at the grandmotherly woman sitting across the waiting area with the beautiful chocolate Persian draped sedately over her shoulders. *It must be nice to have a cat that's yours*, Skye thought.

"Mrs. Thomas," the blond veterinary technician called out as she carefully rounded the corner cradling a tiny bundle wrapped in a towel. "Dr. Blackburn says you can take Buddy home now."

I wish, Skye thought wistfully. The name Buddy still tickled her. Her mother couldn't abide the beer-inspired names their neighbor had given the brothers, so they'd simply been calling them Buddy and Kenny for short.

Skye took the bundle in her arms while her mom paid the bill and learned how to care for Buddy. She stared at the tiny little face, awake but looking somewhat stunned. One side of his face was shaved and swollen, the left eyelid sewn tightly shut. Skye imagined he was winking at her. The little flirt. Didn't he know he'd already captured her heart—and her mom's too?

"How old is your kitty?" the Persian's person inquired sweetly.

"We don't know exactly," Skye answered. "The doctor guessed around three months."

"He's still beautiful . . . and a tough little fellow. He'll be just fine," she said reassuringly. "You'll see."

Skye cradled Buddy all the way home. Even now, and through thick layers of towel, she could feel him purring.

Her mom was talking to her dad on her Bluetooth headset as she drove toward home. "Please stop on your way and buy kitty litter and a box. . . . It's just for a short time while he heals. There's no better option."

Skye could feel the tension as her mother's voice rose.

"They couldn't save the eye. Had to take it out. . . . It was making him sick. . . . If we'd waited any longer, he'd have lost sight in both eyes—and maybe his life. I only wish I hadn't waited *this* long. . . . I *did* try to get the neighbor's permission. He's avoiding me. . . . For all the attention he pays them, I'm not sure he'll even notice. Jinx eats the food he puts out anyway. As long as it's eaten, I don't imagine he'll suspect they're gone. They spend most of their time at our place anyway."

Skye knew her parents disagreed about caring for Buddy, but she'd not had the slightest doubt who would win. Buddy needed help: they'd do what they could.

"Yes, both of them," Skye's mother continued. "They both need the safety of our home. And I don't want to split them up. It'll be good for Buddy to have Kenny with him."

It was settled. Buddy and Kenny were practically theirs.

Buddy didn't seem to miss his eye as much as he missed their home. Just two weeks after the surgery, the hair had mostly grown back and filled in, and he was as bold and friendly as he'd always been. But he'd sit and meow miserably outside their back porch door, pleading to be let in again. Although her dad disapproved, Skye sometimes let Kenny and Buddy inside. It took about five minutes for her to teach them how to go through the old cat door onto the porch, where she faithfully set out fresh water and the healthy cat food her coconspirator, Mom, bought each week with the groceries.

Buddy seemed to get into more trouble than Kenny did—perhaps because of his eye, perhaps because Kenny's longer hair made him look larger and a bit more imposing than Buddy. Mom kept antibiotic ointment on hand to treat his periodic scrapes and scratches.

So it made Skye nervous when the food on the porch stopped being eaten in mid-October. After a few days with no trace of either Buddy or Kenny, she was really worried. One day, after school, she prepared to go searching for the cats. But her mother stopped her with horrible news.

"Gone?" Skye slammed her books down on the table. "What do you mean they're gone?"

"He got a Rottweiler and didn't want cats anymore." Mom looked as upset as Skye felt. "He got rid of them."

"Got rid of them," Skye repeated slowly. "Like, gave them away?" Mom nodded. "Did he take them to the pound? Maybe we could adopt them."

Mom shook her head and pulled Skye into an embrace.

"They're not coming back," she said, rubbing Skye's back consolingly. "He said he gave them a good home on a farm about sixty miles from here."

"He didn't just dump them?" Skye's eyes were wide in horror.

"He said he didn't."

"Didn't he know we would have taken them?"

Skye buried her face in her mother's shoulder. "It's not fair. We loved those cats . . . and now they're gone. It was all for nothing."

"It's never for nothing," her mother soothed. "When you love, it's always worth it. Your investment always comes back to bless you."

I'll never love another cat, Skye vowed. *It hurts too much.*

Skye raced to the kitchen to grab a breakfast bar before heading to school. March had come in like a lamb, so she decided against wearing her jacket and tossed it over a kitchen chair. It was then she heard yowling. *Spring*, she thought dismissively. *He-cats courting she-cats, probably.*

But something in the tone sounded insistent, so she went to the patio door to look. She couldn't see anything, but it sounded close, like the cat was just outside the porch. Her heart beat faster as she opened the door and stepped onto the porch. She expected the sound to send the cat running, but it didn't. Peering through the screen door, she was startled to see a large, disheveled brown spotted tabby—like Buddy, but bigger. Her heart raced. But how could it be? Surely it was a cat that looked like Buddy. He was focused on the blocked cat door to the porch as if annoyed that he hadn't been expected.

Skye pulled the board out of the slot, and in a flash the cat shot inside. He rubbed against her leg and purred. She scarcely dared believe. Was it? He looked up at her, and the winking left eye said it all. It was Buddy . . . *her* Buddy. Her love had returned.

CHAPTER SIX

Cats Love for a Lifetime

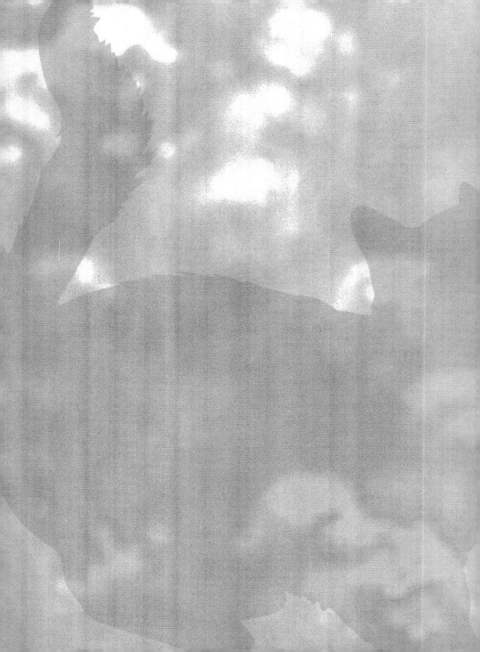

In this world you will face trials and you'll shed tears; but don't lose heart. Joy will return. Love never gives up but always hopes for the best. Love is always patient and kind. And not even death can separate you from My incomparable love.

Forever,
Your Loving God
—from John 16:33; Psalm 126:5; 1 Corinthians 13:4, 7–8; Romans 8:38–39

Creme Puff was no cream puff. She lived thirty-eight years and three days (August 3, 1967–August 6, 2005) to become the longest-living cat ever documented. Other cats have come close: Ma, who died in 1957 at age thirty-four; and Granpa, a rescued Sphynx who was thirty-four years and two months old when he died in 1998, after years of eating an unusual and varied diet that included bacon and eggs, asparagus, broccoli, and coffee with heavy cream. Amazingly, Granpa and Creme Puff were both companions of Jake Perry, a man who must be doing something right.

The average lifespan for an indoor cat is twelve to fifteen years, although there is evidence this may be increasing. And because of better veterinary care, the quality of life and health of your cat even in later years can be better than it has ever been before.

Whether your cat lives for three years or thirty, she gives you the best gift she can offer: love for a lifetime. No matter how old cats get, we can still see the healthy, strong kittens with whom we fell in love. And regardless of how old we grow, cats see our young souls. Our faults, our disabilities, our declining strength matters not to our cats; they'll still look us in the eye, purr contentedly on our laps, and gladly rub against us to claim us as their own. No matter how old they may grow, cats and those who love them always die young.

What greater gift than

the love of a cat?

Charles Dickens

Cat Call

"Wake up, Sleeping Beauty!" a wizened Prince Charming whispered gently, tenderly kissing the white curls that fell across his wife's wrinkled brow. The lines caused by the march of advancing time bothered him not one whit, but these furrows of sadness were something else altogether. Every day Paul tried to kiss them away with love, to coax out her smile with the joys of life, but the shadows of sorrow seemed only to lengthen.

He dodged the arm that flew up to cover her eyes. "Pull the shade!" she commanded grumpily. "It's too early." She rolled deliberately onto her side and pulled the duvet over her face.

"It's not too early," Paul tried to sound upbeat. "It's the best part of the day—your favorite."

She pulled the cover from her face but moved a pillow over her head.

"It's a beautiful morning," Paul continued brightly, raising the shade on the second window. He could see the burgeoning garden through the sparkling glass. He had made a special point of keeping that window spotless so his wife would have no barrier to seeing it plainly.

"Come on, Suzie," Paul tapped gently on his wife's feet through the covers. "Your garden's calling to you. It's time to plant morning glories, collards, and pole beans. Time to pick lettuce, spinach, and peas. Let's get up and get going!"

She groaned but didn't move. The answer was plain: today would not be the day his wife would leave her dark refuge and rejoin life. Paul sighed softly, pulled his garden cap from his back pocket onto his nearly bald pate, and retreated from the room. He left the shades up, however. If she wanted to live out her days in a darkened room, she'd have to get up herself to block out the light.

He pulled rubber-tipped mud gloves carefully over knuckles knotted by arthritis as he headed for the garden. Gardening had been Suzie's special pleasure for years. But then so had the cat. When she'd lost the one, she'd given up the other. Paul had planted and tended her garden, hoping that when the darkness passed, she would regain interest and find it ready for her to pick up again. But he saw no signs of that happening soon.

He glanced wistfully at the engraved granite stone near the patio, the name "Oliver" practically obscured by bright-blooming scarlet dianthus, and the newer patch of dirt beside it, where he'd buried Oliver's son Dodger in March. They'd lost cats before, but it had been a particularly hard, drawn-out struggle with Dodger. For almost a year it had taken both Suzie and Paul to give the large silver tiger cat daily fluids under his skin in an unpleasant procedure that involved a bag of saline solution hanging from a plant hook in the ceiling, a long line of plastic tubing, and a very large needle. In spite of their best care and intentions, Dodger had lost his battle with kidney disease at the age of eighteen and a half. He had wasted away to just a shadow of his former self before finally lapsing into a coma and dying in Suzie's arms.

Paul had wanted to get her a new kitten, but Suzie had been adamantly opposed. "I'm eighty-four years old," she'd said wearily. "I'm too old to start over with a young kitten."

"I'm eighty-five," Paul had responded lightly, "and I'm not too old."

"Oh, Paul," Suzie had scolded. "I'm being serious. What would become of a cat after I'm gone?"

"I promise to take care of him," Paul had said solemnly but with a twinkle in his eye.

"It's not fair to a kitten to bring him into a home where we're too old to play with him and won't be around to give him a full lifetime of love."

Paul had relented. He understood that Suzie's low spirits had as much to do with coming to grips with her own mortality as it did with losing Dodger, especially since she'd been diagnosed with kidney disease herself in the midst of Dodger's struggles. Still, he felt certain a new little kitten to love would help get Suzie's mind off of herself. The dangerous depression that had descended on his wife's mind in recent months convinced him that she had given up and was just waiting to die. It scared Paul.

God, help me find some way to reach her, he prayed as he retrieved the hoe from the shed. *Help her.*

As he closed the shed door, he heard something. Was it just the squeaking of the hinges? He stood still, listening. *Mraow.* The hair on the back of his neck stood up. It sounded like Dodger—that distinctive Siamese cat call that had always seemed so strange coming from a cat who didn't look a bit Siamese. He leaned the hoe against the shed and went to investigate, casting a self-conscious look back to Dodger's grave.

Mraow! Paul made his way cautiously toward the sound in the garden. He could see the asparagus ferns twitch and rustle, as if they felt the same sense of anticipation he did in waiting to see what would emerge. "Here, kitty," he coaxed in the sweet voice he'd used with Dodger as he peeled off his gloves. He was afraid the cat would bolt in fear at his approach, but instead of running away, the cat came toward him. When it emerged from the dense undergrowth, Paul caught his breath and took a step backward. The cat looked like a negative image of old Dodger—where Dodger had been dark, this cat was light; where Dodger was light, this cat was dark. But the markings were eerily similar.

The overall effect was a lighter, ghosted version of Dodger. For a moment the silly idea flitted through his mind that maybe this *was* Dodger's ghost.

The cat came to him, talking nonstop and rubbing against his legs, threading between them and purring loud enough even for Paul to hear. "Don't trip me up," Paul said, laughing. He couldn't get over the cat's remarkable resemblance to Dodger.

Not a stray, he decided, noting the flea collar and healthy sheen of the ghost cat's coat. "Where did you come from?" He debated about calling Suzie out to see the cat. Would seeing Dodger's doppelganger make her happy or cause more pain? He sat on the old iron chair while he considered what to do next, and after a few moments of rubbing its face on his work pants and extended hand, the cat took it upon itself to jump onto his lap. Paul chuckled. "Friendly fella, aren't you?" Then, catching a better view, he corrected himself: "Excuse me, ma'am." He rubbed behind the cat's ears and under the collar. The cat contorted in obvious pleasure. "Would you like to meet someone awfully special to me? I know you'd love her, too."

"Oh!" Paul heard Suzie's voice quivering with emotion as she spilled out the door from the house in her nightdress and house shoes. "I heard . . . I saw . . . Paul, where did you get that cat?"

"She just came for a visit and to help me in the garden," Paul answered as the cat jumped down from his lap and turned to greet Suzie like an old friend.

Paul smiled with satisfaction. He had a feeling Suzie just might have turned the corner.

The next morning Suzie was up before he was and eager to get to the garden. Sure enough, that morning—and most others all summer long—brought the cat they called Sprite to visit them in the garden. Not only did Suzie's health and good spirits grow along with the garden, but Paul was convinced that the cat who loved to lounge in the asparagus patch was a good pest deterrent, bringing them a bumper crop. Sprite usually stayed anywhere from just a few moments to almost an hour, but by the time she left, Suzie was invigorated enough to tackle other projects. They cleaned the basement together, made a huge batch of molasses cookies, canned tomatoes and beet pickles, and even resumed their morning walks around the neighborhood.

As the season changed, so did the cat's habit. She came less frequently, until she came not at all. Still, Suzie seemed to take comfort from Paul's assurance that Sprite had a home somewhere nearby and people who loved her and cared for her during the cold months. She calmly bided her time through the winter.

But when spring came, Suzie was back to the garden as soon as she could stand to work the soil. She said she was just trying to get an early start on the season, but Paul knew the truth: she was looking for Sprite.

Her patience, with time, turned to worry, then panic, and finally despair as the cat failed to return to the garden. Finally, one beautiful morning in mid-May, Suzie wouldn't get out of bed.

Paul walked alone through the neighborhood that morning, grappling with feelings of helplessness and sorrow. What could have happened to that cat? Should he try to find a kitten, or would that make matters worse? *God, help me know what to do*, he pleaded.

Mraow! Paul stopped dead in his tracks. *Mraow! Mraow! Mraow!* The sound got louder as the door to the house on the corner opened and a woman stepped out to retrieve the newspaper.

"Excuse me," Paul called to her. "Is that a Siamese cat I hear?"

"Oh, no," the woman explained cheerily. "She doesn't look Siamese, but by her voice, I'd say one of her ancestors must have been."

"Is she a silver tiger cat, by any chance?" Paul asked hopefully.

"Why, yes." The woman seemed surprised.

"Could I see her, please?" Paul pleaded. "I think she might be the cat who visited my wife's garden last year—it meant so much to Suzie, but we haven't seen her this year, and my wife's worried sick that something's happened to her."

"That's probably Phoebe," the woman said kindly, gesturing for Paul to follow her. "We've kept her inside the past six weeks because she's caring for kittens. They're six weeks old and ready to go at any time. Would you like one?"

"Wake up, Sleeping Beauty," a beaming Prince Charming whispered mischievously as he kissed Suzie's furrowed brow. "Sprite sends her love," he said excitedly as he deposited two furry, squirming kittens beside her on the bed—one looked like Dodger, the other like Sprite.

"They're ours?" Suzie's delight was obvious.

"To love for a lifetime," Paul smiled. "A long, happy lifetime together."

CHAPTER SEVEN

Cats Bring Happy Endings

Don't worry! I know the plans that I have for you. I won't harm you. Instead I'll give you hope and a future. The key is loving Me and being called according to My higher purpose. Watch Me take even the bad things and transform them into unexpected blessings for you. Just keep committing everything you do to Me and trusting Me for true success. Remember, My plans, not yours, bring victory.

Working for your good,
Your God of Happy Endings
—from Jeremiah 29:11; Romans 8:28; Proverbs 16:3, 19:21; John 14:6

Sometimes bad situations turn out better than we'd hoped. Molly had good luck—in spite of the fact that she's a black cat—when she was rescued safe and sound after spending fourteen days stuck in the wall of a New York deli in April 2006.

More than twenty months after his family lost him in a tornado in Nebraska, orange and white tabby Harley made his way back to his owners—the night before their son was to leave for military duty.

In Connecticut, Charlie, a Rottweiler puppy rejected by his mother, was accepted and nurtured as one of her own kittens by a generous and loving cat named Satin.

Difficulties come to everyone. Rejection, disappointment, loss, conflict, pain, loneliness, or even boredom can make us face the future with a sense of dread or fear. Because we're human, our understanding and the scope of our vision are limited. We can't see what tomorrow holds, but we can hold tightly to the One who sees and knows all: "I know the plans I have for you . . . ," God reminds us in Jeremiah 29:11, "plans to give you hope and a future."

No matter what the situation in which you find yourself today, take a cue from your cat. Don't worry or fret about what might happen tomorrow. Don't spoil today with fears of an unknown future. Rather, walk on in confidence and with trust, knowing that someone who loves you is looking out for you and will provide what's needed at the right time, in the right way. God loves to delight His children with happy endings.

Do you see that kitten chasing so prettily her own tail? If you could look with her eyes, you might see her surrounded with hundreds of figures performing complex dramas, with tragic and comic issues, long conversations, many characters, many ups and downs of fate.

Ralph Waldo Emerson

Cat and Mouse

Don't Russians believe in happy endings? Darya pondered, listening to the dismal March downpour and lingering meditatively over the closing lines of *Dr. Zhivago*. When the phone rang, she checked the caller ID to see if she wanted to answer.

"Can you come for dinner tonight?" Heather, her lifelong best friend, said a little too cheerfully. And vaguely—none of the usual chattering about what else was on the agenda. Darya was immediately suspicious.

"Who else will be there?"

"Just a couple of other people," Heather said, evasively, Darya thought.

"Mm-hmm. And these couple of people would be . . . men, I suppose?"

"Oh, Dar, you're such a cynic." Heather paused. "Okay, yes, but I don't think they'll bite." She made a short, frustrated growl. "Really, Darya, how are you ever going to meet anyone if you—well—refuse to meet anyone?"

"I've met a few, and it didn't go so well, if you remember."

"Oh, I know," Heather groaned. "But really, Dar, you've got to get back out there. Life isn't all as grim as your Russian novels."

Darya sighed. "I know you're right. But like Mom used to say, 'Once burned on hot milk, you'll blow on cold water.'"

Heather laughed sweetly. They both had rolled their eyes at Darya's Russian mother's proverbs when they were younger, but now that she was gone, they often echoed them for fun and fond memories. "Funny," she said, "the one that came to my mind was, 'The appetite comes during the meal.' Come on, it's just dinner. He's a professor. Just meet him and see if he seems . . . appetizing," she finished with a giggle.

Darya pictured a dweeby guy in rumpled Dockers and a sweater with elbow patches. "No thanks."

Heather made her last hopeful pitch. "You really might like him. He's into Russian stuff, like you."

"Thanks, Heather, really. But I honestly do have plans tonight." She grinned and talked faster as she shared her news. "I've *finally* located two black Siberian kittens—they're *so* hard to find here in the States—and the best thing is, the cattery's only a couple of hours away, in New Brighton. I'm going this afternoon. I'm so excited! I even have names picked out—Sasha and Katya, after my cousins. I've got to get going before someone else snatches them up."

"I hope *they'll* keep you warm at night." Heather sighed in resignation. "Well, congratulations! I know how much you've wanted this. Go get 'em!"

Darya's anticipation grew the closer she got to the cattery. She'd been searching for a pair of Siberians to adopt since her visit to Russia, when she fell in love with the ones belonging to her relatives. Their beautiful, round eyes and thick, long hair were striking, but it was their affectionate, playful, and unusually outgoing ways that won her over. She'd never seen a cat who would eagerly run to greet visitors rather than retreating under a bed!

She pulled into the parking lot and practically trotted to the door. Inside, a friendly employee greeted her.

"I'm here about the two black Siberian kittens," Darya announced almost breathlessly.

"Ah . . . well, the female is already spoken for, but the male is still available. Would you like to see him?"

Darya was crestfallen. "But I called just this morning . . . and I so wanted both of them . . ."

The elderly woman frowned in sympathy. "Oh, I'm sorry. A man came in just a couple of hours ago and put a deposit on her. But I'd be happy to show you her little brother," she said hopefully.

The male kitten was a glorious, glossy bundle of black fur. He immediately crawled up onto Darya's shoulder and purred luxuriously in her ear. She was a goner, and she smiled in spite of herself.

"Oh, how could I refuse him?" She smiled at the woman. "I'll take him!" But she wasn't quite ready to give up her dream of having the pair. "You said your other customer put a deposit on the female. He hasn't taken her yet?"

"No, he'll be back tomorrow."

"Could you please, please try talking him into waiting for the next litter?" she pleaded with a desperate kind of hope. "So they can stay together?"

The woman looked reluctant. "Well, I don't know . . . I guess it would be nice for them to stay together. But I'm not in the habit of trying to talk customers into *not* adopting one of our cats."

"Please?" Darya said piteously. "I so had my heart set on taking both of them."

After a long moment of indecision, the woman relented. She promised she'd call.

When the phone rang the next morning, Darya's heart skipped a beat. "This is it," she told Sasha, who had taken immediate possession of his new home—and his new person's heart.

Darya held her breath as she picked up the phone. "Hello?"

"This is Evelyn, from the Brighton Cattery . . ."

Darya stroked Sasha, as she listened, and her heart sank.

"Hon, I tried, but this gentleman just wouldn't budge. He was intent on adopting the little female."

Darya's temper was starting to kick in. Why wouldn't this guy just wait for the next batch? How could he insist on splitting up the brother and sister? "Surely there's some way to persuade him," she pressed. She just wasn't ready to give up. She'd felt so sure that this was meant to be.

"He's coming to pick her up later today," Evelyn said kindly. "Come meet him. Talk to him yourself. He's a nice man, maybe lonely. Handsome. You're attractive, not old like me. He just might listen to you."

"No thank you," Darya replied politely. She saw the red flags of a setup, and it made her want to retreat. Her life was starting to feel like a depressing Russian novel. Both cats had been destined for her, she just knew it. Now fate was conspiring to deprive her of her much-wanted kitten while foisting upon her an unwanted blind date. It foreshadowed no happy ending.

Sasha was already showing signs of the large, muscular cat he would become when Darya packed up his special bedding and toys and headed out into the bright autumn day to take him to the pet hotel, where he would stay while she vacationed. As the staff member greeted her and admired Sasha, he commented how unusual it was to have two such rare cats boarding at the same time.

"Really, you have another?" Darya asked, interested.

"She's just leaving. Her person's here to pick her up now." The clerk nodded toward a tall man standing about eight feet behind her, with his back turned, looking out the front window.

Hmm, Darya thought in passing as she noticed his muscular frame and slightly mussed, thick black hair. But she really wanted a look at the pet carrier being brought from a hallway into the lobby. She tried to position herself so she could see into the carrier, but it was turned so she couldn't see the cat inside. She just caught a glimpse of glossy black fur. Backing up a few steps and straining to see, she suddenly tripped over a toy on the floor, lost her balance, and stumbled right into the man at the window, who had turned to greet his feline.

"*Umph*—oh! I'm sorry," she muttered, embarrassed, as he placed one hand on her back and caught her elbow with the other to steady her. "I just—I was—the clerk said you had a Siberian, and I was curious." She felt herself flush as she took in his blue eyes and clean but unshaven look, always her weakness.

"It's okay," he said with a bemused smile. He turned the carrier around with an air of pride. "She's a black Siberian. I adopted her about six months ago."

Darya's heart skipped a beat, and she leaned down closer to the carrier door. Staring back at her was a more petite but perfect image of her Sasha! Here was her long-lost kitten—and this was the man who had adopted her right out from under her! For a flash she felt the old resentment, but Sasha had brought her so much joy that she couldn't be really angry. She must have had an odd look on her face, though, because the man asked, "Is something wrong?"

"Oh, no. It's just—I think you have my Sasha's sister. I adopted him around the same time." She motioned toward Sasha's carrier, where he sat purring and chirping as if he recognized his litter mate.

The man looked at Darya with growing understanding. "You're the person who tried to get me to wait for the next litter?"

She laughed nervously. "That would be me. I'd really had my heart set on adopting both of them. I was going to call them Sasha and Katya, but while I was trying to wriggle out of a lame-o blind date, someone stole her out from under me," she said in an awkward attempt at good humor.

The oddest look came over his face, and Darya was afraid her friendly intent hadn't come through properly.

"Funny . . . I had to stop by the cattery earlier than planned because I had a dinner appointment that evening with friends."

Darya felt her stomach tighten. *Surely not . . .*

"The Prufrocks? Jess and Heather?"

Darya's face froze into a half smile, half grimace. She nodded. "And you're—"

"Your 'lame-o blind date.'" He laughed. "My name is Aleksandr. I'm a—"

"Professor?" Darya finished, wincing apologetically.

"Russian lit." Aleksandr's smile amazed her as much as the Russian lit connection. "Don't worry about it. If something's meant to be, it will be."

"I'm Darya," she said, extending her hand.

He shook it warmly. "Well, Darya. We finally meet. It seems our paths keep crossing."

She laughed. "Maybe more than you know. The woman at the cattery offered to arrange a meeting to see if I could talk you into giving up . . ." She looked toward the carrier at his feet.

"Katya," he completed her sentence with a mysterious upward curl of his lips.

"Katya," she said with a soft smile, "You gave her my name!"

"Why not?" his eyes danced mischievously. "You gave yours *my* name."

"What?" she asked, uncomprehending. "You said your name is Aleksandr."

"My friends call me . . ."

"Sasha," they both finished together.

Darya laughed. "This is starting to feel like a plot from a novel."

"Then we should get together to critique the storyline," Aleksandr said with a smile, "and perhaps some character development."

"You seem eminently qualified," she teased. Suddenly it seemed possible that her Sasha and Katya might finally get together. It was just enough to make Darya believe in happy endings.

*If animals could speak
the dog would be a blundering
outspoken fellow, but the cat would
have the rare grace of never saying
a word too much.*

—Mark Twain

For your friends who love dogs . . .

Stories, sayings, and scriptures to Encourage and Inspire

hugs

for
Dog
Lovers

WILLIE & KORIE ROBERTSON
Personalized Scriptures by
LEANN WEISS

$11.99 ($14.99 CAN)